curiousabout

ROCK CLIMBING

BY KRISSY EBERTH

AMICUS LEARNING

What are you

curious about?

CHAPTER THREE

3

Taking It Outside
PAGE
18

Curious About is published by Amicus Learning, an imprint of Amicus
P.O. Box 227
Mankato, MN 56002
www.amicuspublishing.us

Editor: Alissa Thielges
Series Designer: Kathleen Petelinsek
Book Designer: Lori Bye
Photo Researcher: Omay Ayres

Library of Congress Cataloging-in-Publication Data
Names: Eberth, Kristin, author.
Title: Curious about rock climbing / by Krissy Eberth.
Description: Mankato, MN: Amicus Learning, 2024. | Series: Curious about the great outdoors | Includes bibliographical references and index. | Audience: Ages 5–9 | Audience: Grades 2–3 | Summary: "Questions and answers give kids the fundamentals of rock climbing, including gear, equipment, and competitions. Includes infographics to support visual learning and back matter to support research skills, plus a glossary and index" —Provided by publisher.
Identifiers: LCCN 2023009433 (print) | LCCN 2023009434 (ebook) | ISBN 9781645496649 (library binding) | ISBN 9781681529530 (paperback) | ISBN 9781645496908 (pdf)
Subjects: LCSH: Rock climbing—Juvenile literature.
Classification: LCC GV200.2 .E34 2024 (print) | LCC GV200.2 (ebook) | DDC 796.522/3—dc23/eng/20230316
LC record available at https://lccn.loc.gov/2023009433
LC ebook record available at https://lccn.loc.gov/2023009434

Photo credits: Krissy Eberth, 17; Getty/Aleksandar Jankovic, 11, DieterMeyrl, cover, 1, Don Mason, 5, peepo, 9, rcaucino, 19; Shutterstock/africa_pink, 7, Alex Brylov, 12–13, 14, Alexandru Nika, 6, Ariful Azmi Usman, 15, Bill45, 21, Maria Isaeva, 16, minizen, 22

Printed in China

Young kids can climb
with an adult watching.

Am I old enough to rock climb?

Yes! You can start rock climbing as soon as you can walk. There are even **harnesses** for toddlers! Most kids start at 6 or 7 years old. But you can climb at any age. Rock climbing takes strength and **flexibility**.

Climbing shoes have sticky rubber on the bottom.

What equipment do I need?

First, you'll need climbing shoes. These help you grip the rock. A rope, harness, and **belay device** help you climb safely. Climbers use a crash pad when they are outside. Always wear a helmet when climbing outside. You never know when a rock might fall!

Always check your gear before starting a climb.

What if I'm scared of heights?

It's okay. Many climbers have **overcome** this fear. They begin with easy climbs. You can start with a tall jungle gym. Then climb a short wall at a climbing gym. The more you climb, the easier it will be. Once you get used to it, head outdoors!

DID YOU KNOW?

Most indoor climbing walls are 30 to 60 feet (9.1–18 meters) high.

It takes courage and
experience to climb
an overhang.

How do I start rock climbing?

Most kids start at an indoor gym. Gyms have classes, camps, and teams! A coach will teach you to climb safely. You'll learn how to put on your harness and tie a knot. Teams are based on ability level and age.

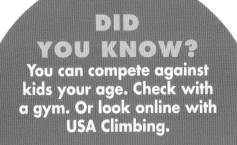

DID YOU KNOW?
You can compete against kids your age. Check with a gym. Or look online with USA Climbing.

Kids start with easy routes
and work their way up.

What will I learn at rock climbing practice?

Heel hooks help climbers get past hard holds.

You will learn about different **holds**. A coach can teach you new moves, too. One move is called a "heel hook." Climbers use their heel to hold themselves up. This gives your hands and arms a rest. You'll also learn training exercises. These build strength so you can climb longer.

PINCH HOLD

A pinch hold is where you pinch the hold between your thumb and fingers.

SLOPER HOLD

A sloper is a hold that uses your whole hand but really doesn't have anything to hang on to.

JUG HOLD

You can use your whole hand to hang on to a jug hold. It's the easiest hold to use.

CRIMP HOLD

A crimp is a hold that only uses your fingertips. It's hard to hold!

POCKET HOLD

This hold has a hole in the middle for your fingers.

How do I compete?

Two climbers
race in speed
climbing.

Pick a competition. There's bouldering, lead climbing, and speed climbing. **Bouldering** is close to the ground. There's no rope or harness. Lead climbing uses a belay. You climb as high as you can without falling. Speed climbing is a race up an indoor wall.

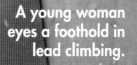

A young woman eyes a foothold in lead climbing.

What knots do climbers use?

There are many! You will first learn the figure eight knot. This knot ties onto your harness. You will also use hitch and anchor knots. These two knots tie the rope to the rock wall. They are used to climb outside.

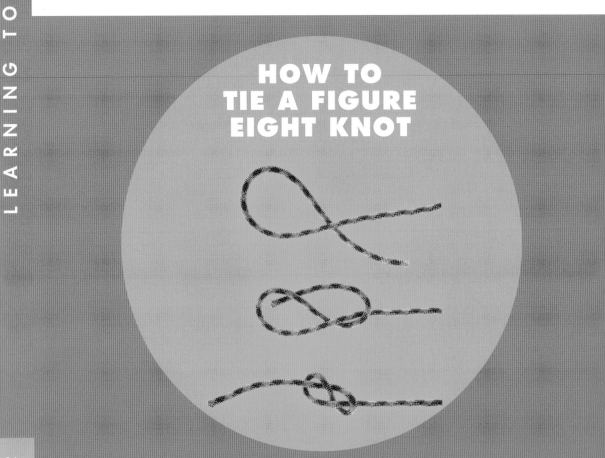

HOW TO TIE A FIGURE EIGHT KNOT

This climber used a figure eight knot to tie into the route.

Is rock climbing dangerous?

No. You may get scrapes and bumps or small injuries. But it is safe when you follow the safety rules. Remember to always check your harness. Check your knots, rope, and belay, too. Wear a helmet. And never walk under a climber.

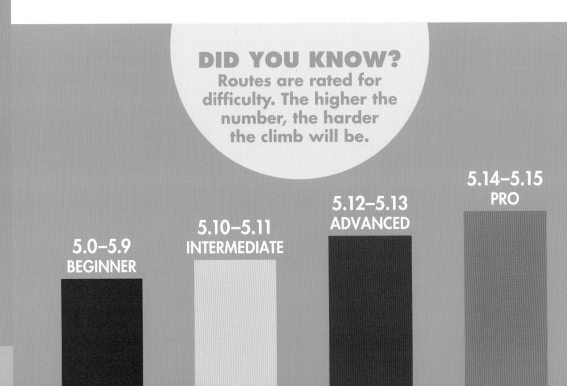

DID YOU KNOW?
Routes are rated for difficulty. The higher the number, the harder the climb will be.

5.14–5.15
PRO

5.12–5.13
ADVANCED

5.10–5.11
INTERMEDIATE

5.0–5.9
BEGINNER

Mont Blanc, a high mountain in Europe, takes two days to climb.

Yosemite Valley is known for its famous climbing summits.

Where do people rock climb outdoors?

Some climb rock ledges in their area. But most people head to a park. Local and state parks have climbing routes. Others plan an epic climb at a national park. Yosemite and Zion are great places. An outdoor climb can take hours or days. But the view from the **summit** is worth all the work.

ASK MORE QUESTIONS

What's the tallest climbing wall?

Why do climbers use chalk?

Try a BIG QUESTION:
How does climbing affect the rock's surface?

SEARCH FOR ANSWERS

Search the library catalog or the Internet.
A librarian, teacher, or parent can help you.

Using Keywords
Find the looking glass.

Keywords are the most important words in your question.

If you want to know about:

- where the tallest climbing wall is, type: TALLEST CLIMBING WALL

- climbing chalk, type: CLIMB CHALK USES

FIND GOOD SOURCES

Are the sources reliable?

Some sources are better than others. An adult can help you. Here are some good, safe sources.

Books

Rock Climbing
by Marie-Therese Miller, 2021.

Go Climbing!
by Meghan Gottschall, 2022.

Internet Sites

USA Climbing
https://usaclimbing.org
This is the official site for USA Climbing. Find information about competitions and climbers here.

Watch 11-Year-Old Rock Climbing Prodigy Brooke Raboutou Climb
https://thekidshouldseethis.com/post/86312669332
The Kids Should See This is a site that shares interesting videos that are safe for kids to watch.

SHARE AND TAKE ACTION

Look for climbing classes at a local gym.

Ask a parent to sign you up.

Plan a climbing trip.

Some climbs take all day. Make sure to plan where to stay after dark.

Teach a friend how to climb.

Climbing is more fun—and safer—when doing it with friends.

GLOSSARY

belay device A mechanical piece of climbing equipment used to control a rope during rock climbing.

bouldering Climbing performed on big rocks outdoors or indoor rock walls without the use of ropes or harnesses.

flexibility The ability to bend easily.

harness A set of straps that are used to connect a person to something, usually for safety.

hold A shaped grip that is usually attached to a climbing wall so climbers can grab or step on it.

overcome To successfully deal with or gain control of something.

summit The top of a cliff or mountain.

INDEX

About the Author

Krissy Eberth loves adventure, especially rock climbing with her husband and two daughters. When away from her writing desk, she can be found skiing, hiking, or biking the trails of northern Minnesota.